How to Not just Survive...

This is Your Proven Formula for Business Success

(And yes, even if your customers are spending less these days)

By **Steve Clarke**

Foreword by Bev James
Managing Director of The Coaching Academy
The Worlds Leading Coach Training Organisation

Copyright © 2009 by **Eureka Sales Solutions**

All rights reserved by the author. No part of this publication may be reproduced, stored in a retrieval system or transmitted in any form or by any means electronic, mechanical, photocopying, recording or otherwise, without the prior written permission of the author.

ISBN: 978-1-4092-8771-1

EUREKA Sales Solutions Ltd
Sales & Marketing Strategies for Business Success

Dedicated to my gorgeous wife, Susanne, who has never wavered in her support for me and everything I do... (Except squash that is, which she thinks I'm too old for, and that it causes all my back problems!)

ABOUT THE AUTHOR

Steve left school when he was 16 with no real qualifications or career path ahead of him. By the time Steve was 18, he was on to his third job and had reached the lofty heights of petrol pump attending on a BP forecourt.

One dark, cold, stormy winter's night as Steve stood in the pouring rain filling another man's car with fuel, he made a decision: things had to change. He wanted to be in the driver's seat, inside the warmth of a shiny new car, not standing in the rain pumping petrol for other people.

This spurred Steve on with his voyage of personal development. He gained a thirst for knowledge and self-improvement. Through the materials he read he discovered the awesome power of goal setting. Within months, he landed his first sales job, and inside a year he was sitting in the driver's seat in the warmth of a shiny new car reflecting on his achievement.

At the age of 19, Steve began his sales career in earnest, selling state-of-the-art office equipment. Just 12 months later he was invited to become a director of the company and was responsible for helping to grow and train one of the country's leading and most successful sales forces in this fiercely competitive arena.

Always looking to lead with technical innovation, Steve introduced Apple products to the company's portfolio. Working predominantly in the high-end printing and publishing field, the company won the accolade of being the country's fastest-growing Apple dealership at that time.

Early in 1990, Steve spotted an opportunity in a completely non-related but exciting field that led him to move to America and set up distribution of a unique European product in the winter sports market. Launching a new product, in fact a new winter sport, in a foreign market was not without its challenges. He quickly developed and honed his media and public relations skills, generating:

- A massive amount of free national print and broadcast media coverage for his fledgling business.

- Exposure with a value of over $2.5m – for free! This included appearances on prime-time national television such as *Good Morning America*, *CBS This Morning* and *ESPN Sports*, plus numerous regional appearances that were then syndicated around the country.

- And huge volumes of national print coverage in *USA Today*, *GQ Magazine*, *Vogue*, *Health & Fitness* and far too many more to mention.

This exposure proved invaluable when the company, having acquired the worldwide intellectual property rights, sought initial investment to fund its early growth. An angel investor was found and the company continued its national rollout.

To spearhead the sales effort, Steve built a national sales force supported by three touring demonstration teams. The company grew. To raise additional working capital and to realise an exit for investors, the company went on to complete an Initial Public Offering (IPO) in 1994.

Exploring potential...

In 1997 Steve returned to the UK as Sales Director for a small IT company specialising in laptop supply and repair. To fulfil his brief to expand the business, Steve explored the potential of providing "outsourcing services" to the insurance industry – more specifically to assist in handling their IT-related claims.

A powerful and enthusiastic communicator, Steve was instrumental in developing an unrivalled, value-added proposition that successfully attracted all of the UK's top 10 insurers to trust their business to his company.

Setting the goal...

In 2003 the company strengthened its market position with the acquisition of its largest competitor. The following year the business was listed in the "The Times Top 100" fastest-growing profitable companies in the UK within the SME sector.

Steve has spent a lot of time over the years studying personal development and more specifically the power of goal setting. At the turn of the century, back in 2000, he set himself a goal to retire at the age of 45. He wanted to be financially independent, secure for the future, mortgage-free and debt-free. Given the position of the business and his personal circumstances at that time, to put it mildly, it was a pretty lofty goal, but he achieved it! In 2005 the business was sold.

Coaching discovered...

Retirement at 45 at first seemed perfect. Having the freedom, time and money to do what you choose is great. However, for someone so obviously driven and enthusiastic, it just wasn't challenging enough and lacked excitement.

So having successfully achieved this big goal, just as he has achieved so many other goals in his life, Steve wanted something to provide him "purpose", something real to get up for each day. This is when he discovered coaching…

Passion for the entrepreneur...

Steve has studied Personal Coaching, Business Coaching, Corporate and Executive Coaching, Neuro Linguistic Programming (NLP) and DISC Psychometric profiling.

Although his skill set applies to many areas of business, his passion still rests with the entrepreneur, and specifically with sales and marketing. He now chooses to spend his time helping other like-minded business owners set and achieve their goals.

He runs regular seminars, training and focused marketing mentoring groups. He also operates as a "Virtual" Sales Director for a select number of clients.

"Your infectious enthusiasm and passion combined with excellent content was inspirational. I will be implementing your recommendations and have subscribed to your mailing list, so look forward to attending another of your seminars in the near future. Thanks Steve."

– David Mears

Web Design, Optimisation & Flash Programming

"I have to say that working with you has been a fantastic experience, I feel that it has helped me to focus my thoughts and energies, but more than that I feel that I have developed as a businessman."

– John Ripsher

Harpers Ltd

"Your marketing strategies are worth their weight in gold, as are all of your other business insights and experiences. Thanks again for making me see things differently."

– Chris Gander

Managing Director

Impossible Access Cleaning Ltd

On the personal side...

Happily married and with five children, Steve keeps extremely busy. Besides home and work, he likes to keep active and engages in a variety of sports activities. He holds a private pilot's licence, is a qualified scuba diver and sailor, and loves tennis and squash but is rubbish at golf (but very keen).

Contents

About the Author iv
Forward 1
Introduction 3
Genuine Passion and Tons of Enthusiasm 10
Niche Markets 16
Products People Want or Maybe Really Need 24
Quality Product 39
Automated Systems and the Least Number Of People 46
Multi-Faceted Marketing Machine 58
Regular Repeat Action Which You Test and Measure 58
Qualified Leads and Conversion Ratios 89
Sales to Happy Customers 89
Test and Measure for Better Results 97
More of the Life and the Business You Want 97

FOREWORD

When I first met Steve Clarke, I was immediately impressed by his drive, determination and what I soon recognised to be his instinctive ability to bring out the best in people. It only takes a few minutes to realise Steve's sincere desire to help people launch and accelerate their success.

Steve has a natural affinity with entrepreneurial business owners, whether seasoned veterans or those about to embark on their journey and with his positive, down-to-earth manner he provides a great many "Eureka" moments.

This is not just another theory book; *How to Thrive Not Just Survive* is full of good grassroots stuff, based on Steve's firsthand practical experience at the sharp end.

Many authors profess to have the secret to making millions, but Steve is living the dream because he put the ideas contained within these pages into action. As a presenter, Steve has audiences captivated; he generously offers nuggets of wisdom that can positively impact the bottom line in no time at all.

Steve has encapsulated all the information necessary for success into this book; the rest is up to you. Don't just read this book, devour it – and most importantly, take action.

It's aimed at the would-be entrepreneur but is clearly a sound wake-up call for the rest of us in business. Listen to what he says and take action because Steve's success formula hits all the buttons, and I believe it to be a blueprint for businesses to follow if they want to succeed. Ignore it at your peril.

I recommend this book and Steve wholeheartedly because he is the real deal.

Bev James

Managing Director

The Coaching Academy

the coaching academy
Training courses that change your life

INTRODUCTION

Vision without action is a daydream, action without a vision is a nightmare

Your success in business is going to depend to a great extent on how you look at things. It will then depend on your vision and the action you take and how you act, in other words – your attitude.

What do you see when you read this...

Opportunityisnowhere

"Opportunity is nowhere"

or

"Opportunity is NOW HERE!"

For those seeing the latter, this book is for you.

This book was written for the entrepreneur, the Small to Medium Enterprise (SME) business owner. In the UK, 99.3% of all businesses have less than 50 employees, and therefore fall into the SME category. These same SME's employ around 12 million people in the UK (approx 58% of the private-sector workforce).[1]

---

[1] Source; FSB 2009

Stand tall small business owners – you are small in title alone!

➢ Profit is King

If you are running a commercial operation, you are in business to make a profit.

Always remember, it's not a rude word – "Profit" is KING. Turnover is easy to see, but you've heard the phrase "turnover is vanity, profit is sanity". If you fail to operate in profit, you risk your business and your livelihood. Fail to operate in profit, and you risk the financial security of your family and that of all your employees.

"**Good news – Success leaves Clues**" Profit is one thing all business owners want more of. However, you can't just have extra profit, at least not directly – sorry to disappoint you. The good news is that there are a number of elements that will affect the profit you make. There are variables that contribute towards the bottom line – <u>improve these variables and you can increase your profit</u>.

In all the companies I've owned or operated, and through talking with business owners around the world, I see consistent patterns, trends and activity. Yet more good news – **Success leaves clues**. Follow the clues and you find the treasure. It should be simple enough, but then why do so many businesses fail so miserably?

People often ask me: What's the secret to a successful business, what's the formula?

It got me thinking long and hard. Could there be a formula? A formula that transcends different industries, products and even service offerings?

I have taken what I know to be true and added all that I've learned from working with some of the countries finest business brains and marketing experts. I have condensed much of this knowledge into my "formula", and I'm going to share it with you in this book!

I've heard people say that they were just lucky to be in the right place at the right time. This could be true in a few instances. However, I prefer to believe that we are all capable of making your own luck. My definition of luck is "being prepared to meet an opportunity". How lucky are you?

Once you set your antenna, your radar, you'd be amazed at just what you see coming your way. If you are not prepared to meet an opportunity, things, people, and events would very likely pass you by and fall into the lap of a competitor who has his eyes, ears and mind open.

I think you will find that irrespective of industry sector, product or service, my formula still applies.

Consistently apply my formula and you will:

- Begin to attract new enquiries like a magnet
- Discover how simple changes to your website could triple your sales

- Access dozens of ways to grow your business whatever market you're in
- Learn how to benefit from automated systems
- Earn more profit with less blood, sweat, and tears
- Know the seven major marketing blunders business owners make… and how to avoid them!
- And much, much more…

So what is my Business Success Formula?

Read on…

This is Your Proven Formula for Business Success

THE BUSINESS SUCCESS FORMULA

$$((GP + TE\ \infty)\ NM + (PPW + MRN) + QP = PO$$
$$AS + LNP = LO + MP = GBM$$
$$MFMM + RRA\ (TM!) = PSL$$
$$QL \times CR = STC + MFMM = STHC \geq 1$$
$$(TM + TM = BR)\ BR = MP + MLBW\ \infty)$$

©Eureka Sales Solutions Ltd 2009

How's that? Simple?

"Hold on," I hear you say. You wanted my secret formula to business success, and I offer you an apparent mathematical formula that makes no sense whatsoever?

It's OK... this is **<u>not</u>** rocket science...

But this is your simple proven formula for business success that will let you thrive not just survive.

Let me break the formula down bit by bit and explain just how this it could unlock the secrets to your businesses success.

Are you ready?

OK.

((GP + TE ∞) NM + (PPW + MRN) + QP = PO

Any guesses before you read on?

This will help you:

(**G**enuine **P**assion + **T**ons of **E**nthusiasm to infinity) **N**iche **M**arket + (**P**roduct **P**eople **W**ant + **M**aybe **R**eally **N**eed) + **Q**uality **P**roduct = **P**erfect **O**pportunity

GP + TE ∞…Genuine Passion and Tons of Enthusiasm to Infinity…

> ## If you're feeling battle weary, relight the fire…

To succeed in business and to attract paying clients to your business or service, you absolutely must have an infinite supply of **G**enuine **P**assion and **T**ons of **E**nthusiasm.

It's not always easy, I know that. Some days are tougher than others to whip up enthusiasm. Everyone would be in business for themselves if it were an easy ride. But do you know what I found as I studied successful business people? They all have a genuine passion for the business they were creating, and an abundance of enthusiasm to see them through tough times. They all had a clear vision of where they were going and the type of business they wanted to build along the way. They had a focus and determination, and they adopted a winning "can-do" attitude.

As I studied entrepreneurial success in more depth, I also began to recognise a consistent character trait amongst successful people. They carried themselves with confidence, with an air of superiority – not to be confused with arrogance or complacency – again, this reinforced the positive, winning "can-do" attitude which I believe exists in successful business people.

The subconscious mind is phenomenally complex, yet it

makes no distinction between destructive or constructive thought patterns. If you fill your head with negativity, fear, doubt, and disbelief in your ability to succeed, your subconscious mind will go to work to deliver this outcome for you. Conversely, feed your mind with positive thoughts, and bingo! Try it.

Test this theory and you'll find it applies to winners in most circles; business, sports, politics or the entertainment industry – it can work for you too.

I found the following verse in Napoleon Hill's best-selling book, *Think and Grow Rich*. If you haven't read it, you must. If you haven't read it for a while, it's worth reading again. There is a verse within the book which I read whenever I find myself doubting my abilities, see how this resonates with you:

If you *think* you're beaten, you are,

If you *think* you dare not, you don't.

If you like to win, but you *think* you can't,

It's almost certain you won't.

If you *think* you will lose, you're lost,

For out of the world we find,

Success begins with the fellow's will –

It's all in a *state of mind*.

If you *think* you are outclassed, you are,

You've got to *think* high to rise,

You've got to be *sure of yourself* before,

You can ever win a prize.

Life's battles don't always go

To the stronger or faster man,

But sooner or later, the man who wins

Is the man who thinks he can!

Don't get me wrong; they didn't all know *how* they were going to get there, not by a long shot.

Take a moment now to remind yourself why you got into business in the first place. What vision did you have, and what vision do you have now for where you're heading? Ask yourself, and be honest; has the vision faded along with your enthusiasm?

So, if you're feeling battle weary, relight the fire...

This is not an option, it's a necessity. Look around you. Are your friends and business associates upbeat and positive? Guess what happens to your enthusiasm if you spend your time in the company of negative people. They'll drag you down; they'll sap all your energy.

You need to mix in the right company.

Establish a support network around you that helps fuel your enthusiasm and relight your passion.

"Establish a support network"

There are local business groups you could join (be careful not to join the breakfast moaning groups, there are way too many of those around). I am constantly amazed by the amount of business owners who are willing to get up at six o'clock on a Monday morning to arrive for a greasy breakfast with the same people who do nothing but moan, moan, and moan again. Do you belong to a Monday moaning meeting?

There are good inspirational books to read, DVD's to watch, websites to visit and so on. Subscribe to good e-mail lists that send you useful and upbeat tips straight into your in box on a Monday morning.

You are welcome to listen in to my regular marketing tele-seminars or attend some of my workshops. You could join one of our Marketing Mentors Mastermind Groups, where like-minded individuals meet regularly to share ideas and tips on business growth – strictly no moaning allowed!

To find out more, visit:

www.yoursalesdirector.co.uk/events

Watch the news once a day to keep yourself informed, but be prepared to turn it off once it starts repeating itself. Most of the news is bad news – you must have noticed that. Doom, gloom, and despondency. Some business meetings and networks can mirror this too, so do be careful.

"100% of your success comes from your attitude."

As I'm writing this, the world is nose-diving into a global recession. The world's banking systems are in meltdown. It's real, and it's a problem on an unprecedented scale. Yet despite all of this, *people are succeeding* in business. Not just surviving the credit crunch, but thriving, growing their businesses in times of trouble and in a shrinking economy.

How? I believe a lot of it is down to– one thing – Attitude.

I have set out below a simple graphic illustration I found to show how your attitude can lead to 100% of your success. The number beside each letter of the word **'attitude'** represents the letter's place in the alphabet i.e. A = 1 B = 2 C = 3 etc.

Amazingly, (don't ask me who on earth had the time to work

this out) add up the value of the letters in **'attitude'** and the total comes to 100. A reinforcement that 100% of your success comes from your attitude.

1	A	Action oriented
20	T	Take responsibility
20	T	Turn negative into positive
9	I	Imitate excellence
20	T	Turn fear into focus
21	U	Uncover hidden talents
4	D	Develop yourself
5	E	Expect the unexpected
100	**Attitude = 100% of success**	**Success**

In life there are three sorts of people, and it's all about *ATTITUDE*.

- **Those that MAKE things happen!**
- **Those that WATCH things happen.**
- **And those that WONDER what happened.**

When the going gets tough, the tough make decisions. Decide which of the three you want to be.

NM...NICHE MARKET

➢ Know your target customer & your niche

I love this topic, and it's one that's so often overlooked. It's a little more complex than some of the other strategies I'm sharing with you, but it's well worth putting up on your radar screen.

Knowing your target customer takes on an even greater meaning when you're selling your products or services across different generations. This requires an informed generational perspective to reach each market effectively. You need to recognize what influences their buying decisions. Not as complicated as it may sound, but it's a fascinating topic that's too complex to go into detail about here and now.

These changing dynamics require changing strategies. In other words, the successful strategies used in the past may not work with today's decision makers. The approach you take and the language you use when selling to teenagers will be vastly different to the approach you take selling to someone in their 50's or 60's.

Does this sound obvious? Or, like so many other business owners, have you not really given it a second thought? Do you just apply the language in your marketing that appeals to you and expect others to be on your wavelength?

Here are some key characteristics of the four groups as they relate to sales and marketing. (It is accepted that these are generalizations.)

- Veterans – Ages 61-84: Led the way toward social change and are now retiring.

- Baby Boomers – Ages 42-60: Grew up with prosperity and are into status symbols. Have high expectations and want to be fulfilled in every aspect of their lives.

- Gen-Xs – Ages 26-41: Are willing to live with less "stuff" to have the lifestyle they want. Their battle cry is "I work to live; I don't live to work."

- Gen-Ys – Ages 6-25: Want to be respected, and technology is an expectation, not an extra. They are very media savvy and team oriented.

Here are just a few tips that could help you in marketing to each generation:

- Veterans: Appeal to their interest in seeking new experiences.

- Baby Boomers: Want a personalized service.

- Gen-X's: They know they are being analysed and sold to, so understand their lifestyle and how they will use a particular product/service.

- Gen-Y's: Respond to their expectation for instant communication. They tend to shop in groups, so there is a need to understand who the decision maker is.

Like I said at the beginning, this is a fascinating subject that with some careful consideration could make a huge difference to getting your message across to people in a way that will appeal to them and massively influence your sales results!

Who is your ideal customer? Take a moment right now to write down below the key characteristics of your ideal **"Who is your ideal customer?"** customer. Include things such as age, sex, marital status, the car they drive, the kind of house they live in, the lifestyle they have, their educational standard, the clothes they wear – the more clearly you can define your ideal customer, the more success you will have.

(Eureka [yoo reeka] expressing triumph

Used to express delight on finding, discovering, or solving something, or on finally succeeding in doing something.)

Use the following space to record your "Eureka" moments.

My Eureka Moments

_____

_____

_____

_____

_____

_____

_____

_____

This is Your Proven Formula for Business Success

OK, so you can now build a better picture of who your customers is, their wants, and their desires.

Do you know why focusing on a specific niche is so important? By niche I mean a particular area of a market.

By definition, a business that focuses on a niche market is addressing a need for a product or service that is not being addressed by mainstream providers. You can think of a niche market as a focused group of potential customers.

For instance, instead of offering cleaning services, a business might establish a niche market by specializing in blind cleaning services.

Why should you bother to establish a niche market? Because of the great advantage of being alone there. Other small businesses may not be aware of your particular niche market, and large businesses won't even want to bother with it.

> *"Marketing* **is what you do to get the phone to ring."**

The trick to capitalizing on a niche market is to find or develop a market niche that has customers who are accessible, and that is not covered by an established vendor already. Having identified your ideal customer, you are able to gain access to them far easier, as you will know where to find them and how to appeal to them.

I trained as a "coach". There are life coaches dealing with personal issues, executive coaches dealing with board members of large organisations, and corporate coaches working with staff and management issues in the corporate world.

OK, these are niches, but truly successful coaches would narrow this down even further. If you're a life coach, what's your speciality? Weight loss, confidence issues, relationships etc? Do you see how this works?

It's the rifle versus scattergun approach. You get to see your target customer so clearly that now you know where to find them. That means you can market to them far more effectively and efficiently.

> **"A *sale* is what you do when the phone rings."**

Let's just quickly clear things up for you with another definition, as I'll be talking all about sales and marketing in this book.

"Marketing" is what you do to get the phone to ring.

A "sale" is what you do when the phone rings.

Guess what? If the phone isn't ringing – no sales! OK, so a lot of you may conduct business online and don't necessarily want the phone to ring, but don't be pedantic, I think you get my point.

Marketing is all about reaching potential customers and through your message and methods converting them to eager prospects. Sales then deliver paying customers and work diligently to keep them as lifetime clients.

> *"I just wanted to thank you for the excellent seminar you ran last week. You covered more in 1 hour than*

> some would cover in a day! Your down-to-earth approach and obvious knowledge made it informative, thought provoking, and left me with lots of action points.
>
> "I have now arranged meetings with suppliers to get more information to enable me to improve my marketing and sales... and on that note you gave definitions for marketing and sales which meant I actually understand the difference for the first time."
>
> – Glenys Chatterley
>
> Managing Director, Morestan Services Ltd.

(Understanding the lifetime value of your clients is also vitally import to your success and a topic we shall visit on another occasion – for now, let's get back to marketing).

By purchasing this book, you've demonstrated that you've recognised the importance of becoming an outstanding marketer. Unfortunately, many business owners see marketing as a necessary evil, an unpleasant task they have to carry out at some point or another.

I hope that you'll see that this is so totally wrong – and very dangerous too. To a great extent, regardless of what you are selling, <u>marketing is your business.</u>

Effective marketing is a whole lot easier than you might think. If you don't know anything about it yet, don't panic because you're not alone. Very few business owners do, even many of those who've been in business a very long time.

But that's all about to change – right now – because I'm about to share with you simple and easy to understand strategies that you can <u>implement immediately</u> to <u>significantly improve</u> your marketing and <u>your profits</u>.

PPW + MRN... Product People Want and Maybe Really need

> ➤ **Do people want your product or service?**

Here's a bit of a twist. I remember always being told in my early days in sales:

"Find the customers need and fill it."

Have you heard that too?

I'd challenge that now.

I'd argue you'll have far greater success if you:

Find the customers want and fill that.

Think about it for a moment. Who gets pleasure from buying what you need, and who'd rather buy something they really want?

Have you got a product that people want or really need? All too often, people will start up in business to sell the services or a product that really only they would want themselves. The business graveyard is full of people who had "great ideas" that no one else bought into. Research your product and marketplace!

If money is tight, you don't need to spend a fortune on research, doing a little yourself is better than not doing any at all. Identify the sorts of people likely to want to buy your product or service and ask them what they think of your idea.

Ask family (be mindful they might not want to hurt your feelings), friends, ex-colleagues, local businesses, Business Links, The FSB… really anyone you can think of. Most people, when asked, like to air their views, and often the people you least expect it from may just give you a gem of an idea you hadn't fully considered in their feedback or ideas.

> **"Find the customers *want* and fill that."**

You might even surprise yourself and find that it is an excellent way of generating business. Whatever and however you do it – do your research.

In the late 80's, the last time markets were in real turmoil and we dived into a recession, interest rates were in the high double digits – remember those days? Well, amidst the doom and gloom I decided to adopt my three killer rules for successful sales:

- **sell something different,**
- **sell differently,**
- **and sell to someone different.**

I stumbled across an opportunity which led me into the interesting world of winter sports in North America. Remember, my definition of luck is being prepared to meet an opportunity. With my eyes wide open and looking for opportunity, I discovered a totally unique product manufactured in Europe, and one that the American market hadn't yet seen. I negotiated the distribution rights to North America and away I went.

Within just a few short weeks of arriving in Denver, Colorado, we were starting to make a mark thanks to some carefully orchestrated and free PR. As a result, we obtained some powerful and high-profile media coverage.

My business partner and I soon became known as the English entrepreneurs "bringing coals to Newcastle" (we were, after all, bringing a ski-related product to the heart of American ski country). One thing that stands out for me above most others is that the Americans love the English accent, and we played on it to our full advantage. We became minor celebrities in our local business community, and as such got introduced to all number of interesting and colourful people.

One of these people, let's just call him Dave, was colourful to the extreme and provides a good example of thinking about what people want or really need before trying to take a product to market.

"Fish don't travel well"

Dave was an inventor. Inventors are just great, and they are some of the best and worst people in business. But they don't *always* have what people want or need, you've only to watch one episode of *Dragon's Den* on TV to realise how true that is.

A few months after moving to Denver, we took up residence in a new condo complex. Word got out that the English entrepreneurs had moved in, and just two days after we arrived, Dave came knocking at our door to welcome us to the neighbourhood.

It very quickly turned out that Dave had a product that he wanted our help marketing. He had invented a fish condo! That's right, a condominium complex for fish. This involved numerous extruded plastic tubes, linking fish tanks at different heights and positions. It was kind of like a hamster playground – you've maybe seen the kind of things that they have in pet shops – only these tubes were filled with water and linking tanks so the fish could swim from tank to tank and visit their neighbours.

We were intrigued, and Dave couldn't wait to show us what he'd invented. But maybe he should have, he ushered us next door to view his amazing product!

It turned out that Dave had only moved into the neighbourhood a matter of days before us. In pride of place in his living room stood the amazing fish condo. Unfortunately, tropical fish are much like fine wine – they don't travel well! On closer inspection of his amazing fish condo, we could see three standard fish tanks linked by plastic tubes inhabited only by dozens of floating dead fish.

Acknowledging the fact that fish don't travel well, Dave said he'd clean the tank, restock it and then asked if we would please come and look at the condo again the following day. We agreed.

He had indeed made some improvements the next day. The tanks were clean, devoid of dead fish and lit beautifully. Each tank had small groups of fish in it. They seemed content where they swam and showed absolutely no intention of moving from tank to tank.

When questioned, he acknowledged that they didn't seem to want to use the extruded plastic tube to move about and see their neighbours.

It just didn't work. Unfortunately, despite his best efforts and prodding the fish, Dave's invention failed on a number of levels. He hadn't proven to me that it was a product that people wanted (the fish certainly didn't). It really wasn't a product people needed, and it wasn't a quality product either, albeit that this was a prototype we were viewing.

The irony of this story? If you Google "fish condo", you will still see people (maybe not Dave) trying to market the concept of a fish condo. I wonder what their sales results look like. If you're reading this and selling fish condos like they are going out of fashion, please call me and I'll gladly write an apology and eat my words.

"PPW MRN + Quality Product? No!"

I can't let my friend Dave go without giving you one more fabulous example of his inventive nature. Another little gem that Dave had designed was an automatic horse feeder.

He had figured out in his own mind that people who have horses also need to have holidays. He explained to me that during his market research he discovered that regular old nags, as he described them, could be quite happily turned out in the field, and providing they had water, they could fend for themselves for a few days, or so he believed.

Thoroughbreds or Arab stallions, as he went on to explain,

could not moderate their own eating habits, and therefore had to be fed measured amounts of food on a regular basis or they would simply gorge themselves to death, never knowing when to stop eating, and you wouldn't want that for your expensive horse now would you?

His automatic horse feeder looked very much like a homemade kind of beach barbecue affair. It was basically an oil drum cut in half and hinged so that it would open and close according to a timer.

All I could picture was that poor horse, midway through its feed having the lid slammed down and trapping its head inside the oil drum at best, and at worst, decapitating the unfortunate animal.

I asked him, "Dave, people that can afford a horse of that nature – do they not have a groom to look after the horses when they go on holiday?"

"Yes," he said rather slowly. "That's been the major problem."

PPW MRN + Quality Product? No!

The concept works. Check out any pet shop, and you will find a cat feeder or fish feeder – these items work.

I'd love to think it was Dave behind these products, as he was only a few degrees off.

Here's another example that proves my point.

My wife recently upgraded her mobile phone. She received the inevitable call we all have from our network providers telling her she was such a great customer that she was due an upgrade. Cheaper rates, new model phone, that was the basic idea.

My wife and I had always said, like so many other people, that we just wished a mobile phone was...well...just a phone. Who needs all those other gizmos anyway, we just want to make calls, right?

She decided to do a little research online and, having recently discovered the joys of downloading music to her iPod, very quickly fell in love with the idea of owning an Apple iPhone. Off she trotted to the nearest store, and as soon as the salesman passed her the phone to hold and explore her love affair with the iPhone began to flourish.

It's so intuitive. It's incredibly user-friendly. A keypad that you can simply type with and a large enough screen that e-mail and texts are a breeze. Maps! – it shows you maps of where you are or where you want to go, bus routes, pedestrian directions – even though she'll never need them. Hundreds of applications that you can download to your phone via a built-in wireless network connection! Aps (as they're known) to let you translate any phrase into any language. TV listings for the week. Google Earth so she can spy on people's houses – all on a phone! She really **wanted** that phone, but did she **need** it?

That evening, when I held the new phone and began to see the benefits of the big screen and its ease of use, I suddenly felt an upgrade coming on too. Once I saw it, I **wanted** one!

The very next day, I made the trip to the same phone shop. I was like a little child at Christmas. I was so excited about getting my new iPhone that I almost broke into a run for the last 50 yards to get to shop. (OK, I did actually run the last 50 yards!)

It was Saturday, and the shop was inevitably busy. I waited patiently while those in front of me were getting served. I must have been waiting 10, maybe 15 minutes, when all of a sudden the office door swung open. There stood a scruffy-looking spotty 18-year-old with his hand in his pocket and with a deep sigh he grunted, "OK, who's next?"

> "Once I saw it, I wanted one!"

I stepped forward, "I'm next I believe." I smiled.

He didn't smile back. He pointed to a little counter with the two seats at it. "Sit down," he said. "What is it you need," he asked.

"My wife got an iPhone from you yesterday, and I'd like the same deal please."

"Eight or 16 gig," he grunted.

"Eight will be fine, thank you. I don't think I'll be needing and bigger than that. My wife got an eight-gig one from yesterday, and it was on a business contract. That's what I'd like to do too please."

"Are you a business," he asked?

"I have a business."

"Do you have a business card?"

"Indeed, I have." I presented him with a business card that

had all my details on. Still without eye contact, a please, thank you, or a smile he started entering information on to the database.

"Have you got a piece of letterhead?" he asked.

"No sorry, I don't. It's Saturday and I'm not in the habit of carrying letterhead with me when I go shopping."

"As it's a business account, I'm going to need to see letterhead," he said very adamantly.

"That's strange, as my wife opened an account yesterday. It was a business account, and she didn't have letterhead. Can you please try again and see whether you can find a way round this on the system."

He turned to his computer screen one more time and tapped away. "Nope, sorry, can't possibly do this without letterhead."

"Really," I said in a rather puzzled tone. "Only a manager managed to do it yesterday."

"Well, that's as may be, but it's more than my job's worth to try and do this and beat the system."

"I'm sorry, I don't mean to be rude, but is your manager here today? Maybe I could ask him and just maybe he could find a way round this again."

"He's not in today, I am the manager of the day. And like I said, it's more than my job's worth."

I was just amazed – bubbling up inside with anger – but absolutely amazed!

Without saying another word. I stood up and walked slowly

out of the store. Did he care? No, not at all. He was demonstrating absolutely zero GP and zero TE. He failed to recognise that this was a PPW, and as a result he made absolutely no sale.

I will never go back, and this story has now been told to dozens, no hundreds, of people. How would you feel if that was your business? Have you got anybody like him in your company? Take a good look around.

I'm a big believer in hiring people based on attitude, not skills. With the right person with the right attitude, you can teach them the right skills. I have no doubt that had I been asking this young 18-year-old technical questions about the phone or the service, he would know all the answers so he may have had some skills, but his attitude stunk.

Despite the experience, I still **wanted** my phone.

I got back in my car, drove to another town and into another shop. This time, to my good fortune, I was greeted by the smiling face of Rob the trainee.

"Good morning, how can I help you today." (Well, that's a better start.)

I explained again how my wife just bought herself an iPhone on a business contract, and I want to do the same thing.

"No problems," said Rob. "Please come and have a seat, and let's get this done for you as quickly as possible."

Poor Rob immediately encountered technical difficulties with his computer, he couldn't log on. Then when he logged on, the system crashed. He smiled. He apologised. He smiled some more. "Bear with me just a minute, Mr Clarke, and I'll get someone that can help me with this." He returned with his duty manager, who solved the problem with a couple of key taps.

Rob the trainee blushed, smiled and apologised again. He began taking my details, making polite conversation in between data entry and more system crashes.

I was patient, and you know why?

1. because I really **wanted** this phone, and
2. because Rob the trainee had **GP** and **TE** to infinity. He was trying his hardest, and he was nice to do business with.

Every problem that came up, Rob found a way round it. I walked out of that shop a very proud owner of a brand-new iPhone, and all because one trainee had tons of enthusiasm and genuine passion and recognised what I wanted.

➤ Stop feature bashing and focus on benefits

People purchase based on the benefits to them. What will they get from your product or service? How will they feel, what will they save and so on?

You have probably heard this before, but people don't by features, they buy benefits.

All too often business owners waste time, effort, and money pushing feature after feature of their product or service and…you guessed it, the potential customers don't care.

Take a look at your collateral materials and your website. If you're a "feature basher", your work consists of flyers, letterhead, ads, and a website, all of which have your logo and company name, a list of things you do or the "features" of your products and your phone number. Are you surprised that no one cares enough to respond?

They don't want you or your products: they want to know what you and your products or service can do for them!

This is often very difficult for many people to get to grips with. Here's a very simple method of uncovering the benefit over the feature of your product or service. Try using; "Which means that..." let me give you an example or two.

"We offer an outstanding customer service (feature), which means that you will have no stress or no worries (the benefits)."

"Our long wheelbase cars have extra legroom (feature), which means that your beautiful wedding dress will look as wonderful when you get out of the car as it did when you stepped in (benefit)."

> **"They don't want you or your products: they want to know what you and your products or service can do for them!"**

Here's an example from a client of mine, with his permission.

A chauffeur service has the latest luxury limousines available for wedding hire and is very proud of the shining lump of metal so they tell people:

"We (oh no, here we go with the "we" thing), have been offering an exemplary service (perhaps a little formal or stuffy) to the

35

wedding industry for over 10 years (so what?) and we (we again) have just added the latest luxury SE Mercedes long wheelbase to our fleet (so what?)," ...and on it will go bashing features and we-ing all over the place.

How about:

> **You've found it**! This could be just what **you've** been looking for.
>
> **No stress! No worries**! (Understanding their concerns) **Your** personal chauffeur will be with **you** in plenty of time for **your** photographer to capture the moment that **you** step into the sumptuous luxury of **your** immaculate S Class Mercedes. (OK, so keep a little technical stuff here for the petrol heads.) The lavish and spacious interior with extra legroom will ensure that **your** beautiful dress looks as wonderful when **you** arrive at **your** venue as it did when **you** set foot into **your** car.

Better? Can you tell the features from the benefits? No feature should be mentioned without the back up and reinforcement of a benefit statement.

So you may need to change your entire mindset. Put yourself in your customers' shoes, see their problems, understand their fears, learn their wants and needs, and then provide the solution to them by way of benefits. That way you can stop selling and let people buy from you.

Take the time to understand your customers, and show them you understand them and their wants and maybe needs. Skott Bentley did, and just look what happened.

"I just wanted to drop you a quick line and say thank you. So many of your strategies now make total sense to me. I have rewritten a lot of my web copy and opened an adwords account. Over the last two weeks my ad campaigns generated so many enquiries that I outsourced the follow-up to a telemarketing company. The net result? An amazing £100,000 in incremental revenue!"

– Skott Bentley

A and S Executive Ltd

➢ Sell the sizzle not the sausage

I love this expression. It stuck in my mind the first time I heard it. For me it's so graphic, and that really appeals to me.

There was an advert on TV some time ago, and it was advertising Danish bacon. Do you remember seeing it? Or more appropriately, experiencing it in fact.

"Dani*sssssshhhhhhhhhhhhhhh*." You literally heard the sizzle. The fabulously tasty-looking bacon (sorry veggies and vegans) frying in the pan, you could almost smell the aroma through your TV set, and you would begin to salivate over the thought of the taste – **the benefits.**

They did not mention **the feature** – a slice of dead pig! Sorry again veggies and vegans, but you see how powerful benefits are versus the feature. Are you buying the sizzling Danish bacon over the dead pig?

➢ Stop we-ing all over the place!

You need to understand and accept that no one is interested in you or your products. That's OK, take a deep breath and let me explain what I mean.

Human beings are only interested in "what's in it for me". Someone once explained this to me saying that all people are tuned into radio WII-FM, that's: What's In It For Me. I've never forgotten it since, I hope you don't either.

Review all your sales copy, including your website, in fact, particularly your website, as it's often one of the most prevalent "we" areas. "We" do this... "we" have been around since... "we" have the greatest...etc. etc. People don't care!

What's in if for them? So what that you've been in business 25 years? What does that mean to them? If there's no tangible benefit to the customer, don't mention it – they don't care.

See where you can **change "we and our" for "you or your"** – talk about and to your customers, not about you and your business.

QP... QUALITY PRODUCT

QP stands for "Quality Product". Note that it is it does not say PP for "Perfect Product". Too many people, and I've been guilty of this too, spend way too much time trying to perfect their product or service rather than getting out there and telling people about it and making sales.

> "Does this ring any alarms bells for you? It should!"

QP is simple. You need to be ready with a **Q**uality **P**roduct that delivers value for money and continually improve and perfect things along the way. Don't wait until you think everything is perfect – it never will be. In the words of Nike... Just do it!

Here's an e-mail I received from a friend recently, sadly he didn't come to me for help before it was too late – **he lost his business due to poor marketing and the resulting lack of sales!**

Does this ring any alarms bells for you? It should!

> From: mathewday
> Sent: 28 January 2009 18:46
> To: steve@yoursalesdirector.co.uk
> Subject: a big thank you
>
> Steve,
>
> I'm rapidly becoming a huge proponent of coaching!!
>
> I trust that you'll be run off your feet in the current climate with SMEs clamouring for your skills, so I won't burn too much of your time. For me, though, I thought I'd share my biggest lesson from 2008...
>
> * It's ALL about the right marketing and getting the sales. It doesn't matter if the company's not running like a finely tuned machine if there ain't no sales!"
>
> Mathew Day

Listen to what he's saying!!!

It doesn't matter how well your business operates or how good your product or service is...

It's all about marketing and getting sales!

It was all too late for Mathew – Don't let it happen to you. You must step up your marketing efforts and you must start today.

➤ Delivering Your Promise

Consistency is more important than earth-shattering brilliance. We are not looking to create what the author Ken Blanchard calls "raving fans" – not yet. You must create and deliver products or services your customers want, at the right quality, on time, with the right profit margin and… consistently.

Whatever your promise is to your customers, deliver on it. If anything, under promise and over deliver. Way too many businesses get this concept transposed, and that's not good!

So this all boils down to planning coupled with quality control and how you track your delivery. So if you're a sandwich shop, don't buy too much bread that leaves you throwing away more than you can sell, but also make sure you have enough to cater for demand so as to not disappoint your customers. If you're a service company or a call centre, ensure you have the correct level of staff to meet your customers' peak call volumes. A missed call is a sale lost, and worse yet, potentially repeat orders lost too.

> **"You must step up your marketing efforts and you must start today."**

Whilst you are planning your stock or staff volumes, you must ensure you maintain or exceed your customers' service expectations so that they come back to you as repeat clients. Poor quality of your product or service could easily make your customers seek alternative suppliers – what's the point in that?

When a restaurant can't get your order right or takes far too long to get the food to your table, how do you feel? What's the point of such a business wasting money on marketing to you when you've had this kind of experience? Your business must master delivery, and that means achieving consistency. As a small business you can often cover a mistake with a smile and a personal apology. But, as you grow, as your staff levels increase, as your customer base increases, what was once a small problem could put you out of business. Be warned! Bad reputations are really easy to spread!

How is your delivery right now? Have you mastered the delivery of consistent quality? Quality that your customers are happy with, which is not necessarily perfection? You must consistently deliver a quality product that people want or maybe really need. What you must keep in mind is that there's no point filling the sink unless you first put the plug in! Don't spend your time and efforts marketing your business if people can fall straight down the plughole because of poor service delivery.

Here's an exercise for you: what are your top ten customer complaints? (List them over the page) OK, so hopefully this could be difficult to compile and maybe the last few are grumbles that would only upset someone like Victor Meldrew or another grumpy old man, but let's shoot to exhaust the list of ten, you can have more on your list if you need them. If you're struggling who should you ask? That's right – your customers, they'll appreciate it, but only providing you acknowledge their issues and resolve them wherever possible.

This is Your Proven Formula for Business Success

My Eureka Moments

Once you have identified the issues, set about making the necessary changes to plug your sink before you turn on the taps.

Combine all of these elements and you have:

PO – a Perfect Opportunity.

Summary

((GP + TE ∞) NM + (PPW + MRN) + QP = PO

(Genuine **P**assion + **T**ons of **E**nthusiasm to infinity) **N**iche **M**arket + (**P**roduct **P**eople **W**ant + **M**aybe **R**eally **N**eed) + **Q**uality **P**roduct = **P**erfect **O**pportunity

- If you're feeling battle weary – relight the fire.
- Know your target customer and your niche
- Do people want your product or service?
- Stop feature bashing and focus on benefits
- Sell the sizzle not the sausage
- Stop we-ing all over the place
- Tune in to radio WII-FM.
- Deliver a quality product, don't wait for perfection

AS + LNP = LO + MP = GBM

Automated Systems + Least Number of People = Low Overhead + More Profit = Good Business Model

> **Automate your systems and procedures**

Just read this equation through and you will understand how simple it is. Your business overheads include the cost of your staff, and so it follows: the least number of people you employ, the lower your overhead costs, the lower your overheads, the more profit you get to keep from every sale – and that's a good business model.

So what about **A**utomated **S**ystems? What can you automate? Well, the fact is that so many of your systems and procedures within the business can and should be automated. Obvious things like your bookkeeping and accounting, purchasing and stock control. But what I want to touch on here are ways and means of automating your sales and marketing procedures.

Before I move on, let me make a recommendation to you of a great book that puts lots of this into perspective. The book is called *The Emyth Revisited*, and it's written by Michael Gerber. The book is in essence why most small businesses don't work and what you can do about it. It describes very skilfully the various stages businesses go through during their growth from infancy to adolescence and on to maturity.

"So what about Automated Systems?"

So, I want to add a caveat here, and that is: whilst I say, automated systems and the Least Number of People = Low Overheads, more profit and a resulting good business model, be aware that Least Number of People without automating systems results in your nose being placed firmly on the grindstone with no respite. This is a business that owns you, instead of the other way around, and it's not where you want to be.

You should be looking to automate enough of your systems and procedures to become a true turnkey business. You may well find yourself needing to employ key personnel in order for your business to grow, and Michael Gerber's book talks about this in detail. In fact, if you want to grow your business, it is vital to understand how to automate your systems and procedures so that others can step into your shoes.

An awful lot of people, and you could be one of them, are technically adept at what they do. There comes a point in time when the person doing the technical work is fed up doing the work for someone else and figures they should set up in business for themselves. And in doing so, they make one fatal assumption, and that is believing that if you understand the technical work of the business, you understand how business works technically, and that simply isn't true.

I don't propose to rewrite Michael Gerber's book within these pages. Therefore, if you're currently a hairdresser and want to open your own a salon, or you're a pie maker and want to own a pie shop, read his book so you know what you're getting into. (My wife just read this paragraph, and said that it sounds like I'm suggesting someone opens a Sweeney Todd Pie shop, not the case – I will lend her my copy of the Emyth.)

Throughout this book, I want to offer you real, practical, and simple solutions that will help you grow your business from a sales and marketing perspective. So let me make a couple of very simple suggestions right now that you can introduce into your business to help automate your systems with the least number of people possible (at least people on your payroll that is).

➢ Auto Responders

<u>Embrace technology.</u> Later in the book I am going to talk about your websites and e-mail, but now I want to whet your appetite just by mentioning auto responders. Are you aware of auto responders and the power they have to help you with your sales? Let me explain.

What is an auto responder? An auto responder is probably one of the most important marketing tools you can have if you are doing business online. In fact, I would go further: it's a vital marketing tool that will help you automate your business.

In simple terms, an auto responder allows you to build rapport and communicate with your prospects and your customers via e-mail.

The best part of all, it does it on autopilot.

Most of us know that with simple tools such as Google

analytics you are able to determine the amount of traffic your website generates. However, how many of you actually know who your visitors are? Don't you think that would be a good thing to know? Of course it would.

Imagine this ludicrous situation: you invest in beautiful retail premises, and you invest in merchandising materials and inventory. Your advertising campaign has generated a huge amount of interest, and you just know people will be lined up at your door when you're ready to open.

You're up bright and early on the morning of your first opening. You turn off the alarms and unlock the doors. But before the first customer sets foot over the threshold, you remove yourself to a dark corner of the room, put on a blindfold and gag your mouth.

The doors then fling open and crowds of people descend upon your shop like a plague of locusts. You can hear footsteps, and lots of them, and you know there's excitement. All day, judging by the foot traffic and visitors, you've had a veritable feeding frenzy in your shop. As the last visitor leaves your store and closes the door, you get to remove your blindfold and your gag. You look in the cash register, but there's only a measly few pounds in the draw. It can't be right you think, you had so many visitors.

What happened? Many of them were just looking, that's what. People are only ready to buy when they're ready to buy – not when you're ready to sell.

So what can an auto responder do for you? It removes your blindfold and your gag! Can you imagine how much more

49

powerful it would be to not just know that you've had traffic to your site, but to know who actually visited? That's what an auto responder can do for you.

"So what can an auto responder do for you?"

Your website needs to be set up in such a way that you can collect contact information from every qualified prospect that visits your site. I wouldn't suggest this is done by simply offering a newsletter – people are really tired of that concept. You need to consider what information you can give to the people that will be visiting your site. It needs to be free of charge and of real value for that person to give you their e-mail address and name in exchange for your report or information.

Don't panic, creating a report doesn't have to be an onerous task. If you're a garden centre for example, you or one of your staff can certainly produce a short report that will be of real benefit to a visitor to your website. A report for example on "The top five essential tips when gardening in spring", or "The top 10 tips for keeping your garden in the best shape in summer". You get the idea... provide something that someone who has come to your site because they are interested in gardening will want because it's free and of interest to them. Don't be tempted to try and sell it. Be prepared to give away something with perceived value because it will allow you to start to communicate with that person and earn their trust.

Once you have their contact information, with their permission you begin to build a relationship until you reach a point where they are ready to buy. The real beauty of auto responders is that you create a series of e-mail's just once. You determine the time lapse between each of the series that you want to send out and then forget all about it. Whenever somebody signs up for your report from your website, the auto responder will, as the name suggests, automatically respond by sending the number one e-mail in your series. On the due date for the next e-mail, you don't need to lift a finger, the auto responder kicks in and sends e-mails for you while you're asleep or at work on other projects – **A**utomated **S**ystems with the **L**east **N**umber of **P**eople!

Don't get me wrong, e-mail is not the marketing panacea; it is, however, a weapon you must have in your armoury if you're to compete in today's marketplace and to make your website produce results.

Very few people buy on a first visit to a website, so your best plan is to drip-feed information to them. Keep in contact, build a relationship until they are ready to buy, and when they are you are the person they know and choose to come to.

"The rain makes a hole in a stone, not through violence, but by oft falling"

– Lucretius

Roman philosopher 55 BC

(Lucretius – Now there was a guy that knew all about **RRA**, keep this in mind – I'm coming to this in the next chapter)!

➢ VA's and answering services.

Not every small business owner can afford the luxury of a full-time Personal Assistant (PA). All too often, the business owner is quite literally the front of the house, the head cook and bottle washer. But ask yourself, where is your time, as the business owner, best spent? What could you be doing that will generate the most profit for the business? How will you grow the company if you have to complete every task?

Why not outsource certain tasks to a **V**irtual **A**ssistant, (VA)? There are many professional VA's available to speak to that would be a great fit for your business. What do you outsource to a VA? Well, it is not just what you would call mundane administrative tasks. Think about what essential activities you currently undertake whilst running your business... which of those do you find draining and limit your productivity? This could be anything from handling your diary, managing your clients to helping you with online marketing. Whichever of those tasks are taking up your valuable time, they are the tasks to outsource to a VA...NOW! If anything else, just think about what an hour of your time is worth to your business, even more reason why you should be working smartly **ON** your business and not **IN** it. Your VA should be able to help you focus on your core business vision and ensure that she or he is working with you with the relevant activities to help you achieve it.

Carmen MacDougall of The VA Coaching and Training

Company (www.vact.co.uk) trains high-calibre VA's and helps match entrepreneurs with their ideal VA through her own VA business Smart-Sec (www.smart-sec.co.uk).

To ensure you continue to focus on your core business growth activities, you can also hire other professionals such as a Virtual Finance Director, a Virtual Solicitor or a Virtual Sales Director. Indeed, I operate as a Virtual Sales Director to a small number of select clients. I am called upon as needed to create a sales and marketing plan, to recruit and train a sales team, initiate marketing campaigns, create or review marketing materials etc. etc.

You are able to hire in a specific skill set for a specific task or ongoing part-time support, and only when you require it.

Hiring virtual assistants who work from their own premises can save you around half that of taking on in-house or part-time staff. You get the efficiency and convenience of short-term cover if you need it. The biggest bonus of all is that you only pay them for the time they work. You are essentially hiring them by the hour, but they're not on your payroll.

As a small business, what happens when your phone lines are busy or your office is left unmanned for any period of time? I often ask this of business owners. The answer is invariably the same – we have voicemail or an answering machine.

If you are looking for a product or service and you want an answer to your questions quickly, are you prepared to leave a message on an answer phone, or do you hang up and dial another company? More than half of us would hang up and try somewhere else.

This is a simple solution you should consider. It's efficient, cost-effective, and can be set up in minutes. You'll never miss another call again.

A good answering service (I use www.alldaypa.com) provides businesses from all sectors with a live UK-based telephone receptionist who answers their inbound calls exactly as if they were based in their office.

> "Ditch the answer phone and adopt a policy where calls are personally answered – you'll see results in no time at all."

They can take messages for you when you are in a meeting, out of the office, or simply need a break from a ringing telephone. The messages can then be sent to you immediately via e-mail and SMS so that you can prioritise your workload. They also store all of your messages on your own 'online office', which can be accessed online from anywhere in the world.

Their VA's have all of the information they need to answer your calls. Each call is answered how you want it to be answered and all of the information gathered on the call is sent through to you.

It's a cost-effective way to keep your phone lines manned by a live operator 24/7/365.

Consider the benefits of a good answering service:

- **Keep overheads low** by eliminating the need for additional employees and save office space and costs of additional business equipment.

- Give your customers the impression of a larger, fully manned office **enhancing your company perception.** Years ago a sales manager of mine told me to "fake it till you make it". I always disliked that phrase intensely. It smacked of sharp practice. Although sometimes it's kind of what you have to do in order to give the impression that you're in the same league as some of the big boys, until that is you've earned respect and trust through what you can deliver. At a seminar a some while ago, I listened to one of my mentors, Peter Thomson, discussing this same point. He introduced a new word to my vocabulary, and that word was "verisimilitude". The dictionary definition of verisimilitude is to give something the appearance of being real true – now isn't that better than "fake it till you make it"? Now I feel it's totally acceptable to use a service such as alldaypa not only to improve your service and support, but to give the appearance or comfort to a customer or prospect that you are perhaps larger than you are until they get to know how good you really are.

- **Maintain your professionalism** with highly trained, friendly VA's you can trust as your own.

- Enables you to **concentrate on managing your business** without missing out on any new business opportunities.

- **Eliminate training and recruitment costs.**

- You are open **24 hours a day, 7 days a week, 365 days a year.**

- Services such as alldayPA are human services, your

clients will never hear an answer machine or engaged tone.

Don't miss another enquiry. Ditch the answer phone and adopt a policy where calls are personally answered – you'll see results in no time at all.

Automating your **S**ystems wherever possible will eliminate human error, improve efficiency with the **L**east **N**umber of **P**eople and result in **L**ow **O**verheads. This will result in **M**ore **P**rofit and that has to be a **G**ood **B**usiness **M**odel.

SUMMARY

AS + LNP = LO + MP = GBM

Automated **S**ystems + **L**east **N**umber of **P**eople = **L**ow **O**verhead + **M**ore **P**rofit = **G**ood **B**usiness **M**odel

- Automate your systems and procedures
- Auto responders
- VA's and answering services

MFMM + RRA (TM!) = PSL

Multi-Faceted Marketing Machine + Regular Repeat Action (Test and Measure!) = Pipeline of Sales Leads

> **Are you one of those that proudly boast that you get all your business from referrals?**

If your business runs, as described above, generating all its leads from referrals, that might seem great on the surface, you might even feel proud of the fact. However, if you are to thrive not just to survive in our new economy, you must wake up to reality!

We are living in the information age where despite a referral from a happy customer, your competitors are only mouse click away from your prospects at all times. Besides that, are you really aware of exactly how people portray your business when they refer people to you? In fact, when you stop to think about it, it's a very high-risk strategy to rely entirely on virtual strangers to do your marketing for you, isn't it?

Now, more than ever, you need to become a marketing expert if your business is to thrive. Your business needs to become a Multi-Faceted Marketing Machine. Don't let yourself become over dependent on one particular method of marketing.

You need to learn to juggle, and learn to spin plates. It's fun, much more fun than waiting on referrals alone! The more you practice, the easier it becomes. The key is to become a **M**ulti-**F**aceted **M**arketing **M**achine and add to that **R**egular **R**epeat **A**ction, (Remember old Lucretius, the Roman philosopher? *"The rain makes a hole in a stone, not through violence, but by oft falling."* Not one big hit, but lots of little things over and over again.) All the time you **T**est and **M**easure, that's where you build your **P**ipeline of **S**ales **L**eads.

"If you are to thrive not just to survive in our new economy, you must wake up to reality!"

Here are my top 10 areas to implement no cost or low-cost marketing strategies that will set you on your way to becoming a **M**ulti-**F**aceted **M**arketing **M**achine that will thrive, not just survive.

- Your Website
- Auto responders and e-mail
- Invest in PPC
- Direct mail
- Business cards
- Referrals
- Joint Ventures
- Networking

59

- Press and PR – be the expert
- Testimonials

➤ Your Website – What's its purpose?

Here's one question I'm asked repeatedly, so I thought I would share it with you here in the hope that it will help you improve your performance too.

The question is this: How can I make my website more effective?

OK, so that's a pretty big question. My first response in each case is to ask: "What would 'effective' mean to you? What do you want it to do?"

In the early days of the Internet, we all believed that the purpose of a business website was to have it act as our corporate brochure, right? Take a glossy brochure or product literature and turn it electronic, stick it on the web and let people read it.

Maybe going electronic saved a little on printing costs, it certainly let the "little guy" appear more like the "big guy", (more of my "verisimilitude"), but not a lot else.

If that's the effect you really want – then without being rude – you probably shouldn't waste your time by reading this book any further.

The cold hard truth is that 90% of websites are disastrous. Sorry, but it's true. I don't mean visually. Many web designers do a great job of making websites look quite fantastic visually. The problem is, and I mean no disrespect to the designers, after all they're designers not marketers, most sites just don't perform.

"How can I make my website more effective?"

So when I'm being asked by people: "How can I make my website more effective?" what they're really saying is, "How can I get more visitors, and how can I ultimately generate more sales using my website?"

Does this ring any bells with you? How well does your site work for you currently? What is the purpose of your site? What do you expect it to do?

Not enough people calling or ordering directly? It's OK, you're not alone.

Did you know that less than 1% of people who visit a typical website actually purchase or make contact with that business directly? You read that correctly – less than 1%!

Imagine having a retail shop were only 1 out of 100 people that walk through your doors purchase from you or even have a conversation – how depressing.

There's good news though; there are simple steps that you can take to dramatically improve the potential that visitors to your website will become customers.

First, it's important to understand there are two types of websites I'm talking about.

1. Sales website = arrive and purchase
2. Lead-generation website = arrive and enquire.

Even though your business may involve the sale of anything from photographic equipment, garden machinery, to cosmetics, I urge you to develop your site as the second option – a lead-generation website.

Are you ready for this? The secret to having a successful website today is *not* to make selling your product or service the principal focus of your website. Remember, people buy when they're ready to buy, not just when you're ready to sell.

Instead of trying to sell immediately, focus on giving visitors good information for free – something of real value, for free.

OK, that may sound nuts, and I accept that.

But this proven method is one of the most important shifts we've seen in Internet marketing this century. It could transform your business. It's not uncommon to see a steep change in results by 1200% or more. By the time they are ready to make their purchase, you will have become a trusted source of good and relevant information to them, and you will be miles ahead of your competitors.

You need to start thinking about how you can build relationships with visitors to your website. Shift your thinking from how can you clinch a quick sale to how can you begin to build a relationship with each visitor to your website.

In order for you to begin building a relationship with potential clients, you must open a dialogue, and in order to have a dialogue, you need their contact information. So <u>whenever someone arrives on your website, your primary aim should be to obtain their name and e-mail address</u> at the very least.

What have you got that you could offer for free? I would suggest you look beyond the standard "Sign up now for our Newsletter" scenario. Quite often these are just... well...dull.

You're the expert in your field. You know the kind of things that visitors to your website are interested in. What could you offer a downloadable "Free top tips report" on? Could you offer information recorded onto a CD or even a sample of your product? But remember, you must make the offer so compelling that even the casual surfer is persuaded to stop long enough to give you their name and e-mail details providing what you're offering is of interest to them. Once you have this information, the relationship can begin.

> **"You will be miles ahead of your competitors."**

Adding a sign-up form to your website is a simple process. Talk to your Webmaster or web designer about the addition of an auto responder. They should be able to help you.

Unfortunately, some people are reluctant to share such useful information about their products and services freely, figuring that people will take the information and never actually become customers. OK, so that's true in some cases, but building relationships, building trust, and building rapport are more important than a quick sale to me.

This is precisely why I continue to send out my top tips for business success free of charge. However, all these tips and strategies are just the tip of the iceberg – there's so much more we could do together.

A client recently likened my free tips to ordering a takeaway from their favourite restaurant. The food is still good, but the experience just isn't the same as enjoying the atmosphere and the setting within a fine dining restaurant where the food is delivered to your table piping hot and beautifully presented – altogether it's a more rounded and pleasurable experience. Attend one of my seminars or training days and OK, the food might not be brilliant, but the beneficial gain from the experience of being in a room of like-minded people will let you see that my e-mail tips are really just a good takeaway.

Oh yeah, one more thing with your website. <u>Remember,</u> stop we-ing all over the place! Think WII-FM. People don't care about you; they only care about what's in it for them.

➢ Auto Responders and E-mail

An auto responder is probably one of the most important marketing tools you can have whether you're ultimately making your sale online or offline.

In fact, there's probably only one thing more important than an auto responder, and that's your opt-in list. But as you may well know, auto responders and opt-in lists go hand-in-hand: the list doesn't exist until your auto responder mailing list starts filling up with names and e-mail addresses!

<u>An opt-in list</u> is simply your database of prospects and customers that <u>have agreed to receive e-mail</u> from you. This avoids the risk of your e-mails going straight to your prospect's junk mail folder and being treated as spam. **Never** be tempted to run your e-mail campaign through Outlook.

Never be tempted just to spam. The US has very strict laws regarding spam to regulate commercial e-mail, and it's almost certain that the UK will follow suit. Quite apart from that, it's just bad practice to add people's details to your database without their permission.

To build your e-mail list, have your Webmaster place sign-up forms on each relevant page of your website encouraging people to give you the details and opt in to receive mail from you. The easiest and **fastest way to gather e-mail addresses is to give things away for free**: give away an e-zine (a part-promotional, part-informational newsletter or magazine distributed on the Internet), free reports, free e-books, free access to private websites, or anything else that you can think of. Don't be tempted to offer a conditional giveaway such as a discount voucher that's only redeemable when they purchase one of your products. FREE means no charge. Don't create barriers to getting people to opt in.

Have you noticed on some e-mails that you receive there's sometimes a footnote that suggests: "Send this e-mail to a friend"? This is a great way to generate new leads with little or no effort by having your happy customers or subscribers forward your information to their friends.

Your goal is to get people to sign up to receive that freebie, and to agree to receive e-mail from you in the future! This way, you create a win-win situation. The person that's subscribing gets a freebie, and you get his or her name and e-mail address, and most importantly, **permission to e-mail them in the future.**

You **MUST make sure to include valuable information** in

the e-mails you send, or you will have people dropping off of your auto responder mailing list like flies!

A popular auto responder I use is www.aweber.com, and there are many others that offer various additional features. You might want to look at www.constantcontact.com, or www.infusionsionsoft.com if you are looking for a full Customer Relationship Management solution (CRM).[2]

As I said, auto responders and e-mail marketing are not a panacea. However, one of the leading permission-based e-mail marketing services, Constant Contact, found that 80% of retailers saw an increase in sales directly attributable to the use of e-mail marketing. And get this, of that 80%, 20% reported that e-mail marketing improved their sales by up to 50%. They went on to explain that the average order was of a higher value per customer – we would all like to see that now, wouldn't we?

> **"Make sure to include valuable information."**

Businesses using e-mail marketing report that it's very easy to see a direct correlation between an e-mail shot being delivered and a spike in visitors to their website. So remember, make sure the website is full of benefits – don't waste the traffic.

Keep in mind that hundreds of e-mails pour into people's inboxes every day. Your challenge is to make sure that your e-

---

[2] Jargon – Customer Relationship Management (CRM) is a business philosophy involving identifying, understanding and better providing for your customers while building a relationship with each customer to improve customer satisfaction and maximise profits. It's about understanding, anticipating and responding to customers' needs.

mail gets opened. Here are several key factors to help you succeed where others fail.

1. I've mentioned this already, but I'll mention it again. **Get permission** to send people e-mail. Obtain opt-in commitments from new prospects before sending them e-mail marketing materials. At the end of your e-mail. You must also provide the facility for people no longer wishing to receive e-mail from you to unsubscribe or opt out.

2. As with any marketing campaign, you must clearly **define your target audience**. What do they want, what might they really need, what problems have they got that your product or service will solve?

3. **Grab their attention!** The subject line of your e-mail must be compelling enough to make people want to open your e-mail and feel safe in doing so.

4. **Be sure you are spam-filter friendly.** Because of the multitude of junk mail being circulated around the Internet, spam filters have become far more sophisticated about weeding out what is deemed to be junk mail. Use the wrong words in your headline and even in your copy and away you go… straight to the junk folder, never to be read. Professional e-mail marketing software, like Aweber, or constant contact will check your e-mail before you send it to establish its deliverability against spam filters. Where possible incorporate the name of the person you're sending it to in the subject line. This can often tell the filters that you know the person you're writing to and so avoid your message disappearing into dreaded black hole of a junk folder.

5. **Don't send Incognito.** The "from" line of any e-mail still remains the primary decision factor for people to open or delete messages without reading them.

6. **Get straight to the point.** Your subject line gets attention. Start your message with a clear headline that is full of benefits to create immediate interest. Use short and concise bullet points to build desire, and end your e-mail with a call to action. What is it you want the recipient of your mail to do next? Tell them clearly what to do and how and when to do it.

7. **Don't stand on ceremony.** Be professional but informal. Keep your copy as light and as conversational as possible. Don't go flat out to impress people with your command of the English language or your extensive vocabulary. Your e-mail should read as if you were talking directly to that person, even though you may be sending the same e-mail to 10,000 people at the click of a button.

8. **Don't confuse your message.** Stick to promoting one item or event per e-mail. If this is difficult because you have a range of products and services that are inseparable, make the purpose of your e-mail to get people to visit a separate dedicated landing page where you can then provide all of the relevant information.

9. **Send a test message.** Please, before you send your marketing message to 10,000 people, check the content, the layout and check it works. Programs such as Aweber let you test your e-mail in HTML and plain text before you commit to sending it.

10. **Follow-up.** Have your next follow-up message planned and prepared. Integrate your e-mail with other direct marketing strategies such as direct mail or telesales, but whatever you do, **follow-up.** If you're not following up, you run the risk of leaving 98% of your business on the table for your competitors – I'm going to cover this in more detail shortly and give you some statistics that will scare your pants off!

➢ Invest in Pay Per Click (PPC)

To keep ahead of your competition and to drive your business forwards, you must aim to become an expert in all areas of marketing, both online and offline. I would suggest that one key element of your online Internet marketing strategy should be PPC advertising, and particularly on Google.

I'm assuming it's a given that you know who and what Google is, but just in case you've been abducted by aliens for the last 10 years, Google is one of the most popular search engines on the planet. Every hour of every day millions of searches are conducted on Google. This tells me that if you're going to buy ad space at all in any shape or form, then taking advantage of Google's PPC service is the right thing to do for so many businesses.

PPC, as it's known, is probably the most powerful breakthrough in marketing in decades, yet very few business owners seem to fully understand its power.

Utilizing PPC advertising, you can reach an audience anywhere in the world who has an interest in what you have to offer, and more to the point, people who are looking for it right now! In fact, I would take a bet that right now, as you're reading this, there are people on Google looking for what you have to offer – are they going to find you or one of your competitors?

Google have made it really easy to get started. They provide easy-to-follow and very extensive help with things like structuring your campaigns, writing adverts and creating your list of keywords, and the all-important testing and measuring.

"Just in case you've been abducted by aliens for the last 10 years, Google is one of the most popular search engines on the planet."

Keywords are simply the words and phrases that people type into the Google search bar whenever they're looking for something, and it is these keywords you use in and behind your advert in order to be found. When you first set up an ad campaign, Google will even take a look at your website, establish what products or services you have on offer and then suggest the most appropriate keywords for you to use in your PPC campaign.

If you are in the business of selling good old "widgets", then you could easily set up an ad words campaign so whenever someone searches for "widgets" on Google, your ad appears on the first page – that's relatively easy.

However, if you just use the keyword "widget", you will spend a lot of money with people clicking your advert who only want to buy "cheap widgets", where your products may be "luxury widgets". So, you need to spend some time brainstorming and writing down every permutation and possible phrase that you feel someone would use when searching for your type of product.

Within Google adwords there's a built-in keyword generation tool to help you, you just need to get started. There are also many other keyword services available, such as www.wordtracker.com.

As you become familiar with Google adwords and PPC advertising, you will start to realize its amazing power and potential. For example, the next step on is to take advantage of its ability to specify what is called the keyword match type. This will allow you to optimise your ad campaigns fully. However, I don't propose to take all of your time teaching you all of the finer points of pay per click advertising right here and now. There are entire books written on the subject, and numerous websites and blogs that will help you too.

You can even target your ads to appear within a very tight geographical area too. So if you only want customers within a 50-mile radius of your office to see your ad, you simply set that parameter up as you create your advert.

When people search on Google for your product or service, you need to be listed on the first page of any Google search. Who do you know that goes to page three, four, or five? To achieve this "organically" through search engine optimisation (SEO) can be a bit of a lottery, expensive, and time consuming. PPC can get you on the front page, quite literally, in minutes and at a fraction of the cost.

However, as I mentioned above, there is no point having your ad appear on the front page if it's appearing before the wrong audience and just costing you money to prove the process works. As with any effective marketing piece, it's as much about repelling the wrong people as it is about attracting the right ones.

Through these small classified type ads, you have the ability to direct people straight to your website. These small ads appear at or near the top of the search engine results when prospects do their search on Google. Best news of all, you only pay for your advertising when someone actually clicks on your ad, hence "Pay Per Click". You also have the ability to turn your ad on and off and fine-tune it at will. Turn on the tap, leads pour in. Turn off the tap, convert the leads and repeat the cycle.

Google your product or service today and see the results. Look to the right-hand side of the screen and the results listed there are the PPC ads. If you're serious about succeeding in business, you must test out PPC.

There's even free software available that will let you see what "keywords" your competitors are using, how much they're paying and lots, lots more. One of the key features of PPC is that it's totally quantifiable and measurable. You can test and measure the success of one ad campaign against another, continually fine-tuning to improve results.

Stop wasting your money on advertising that doesn't work; remember, you can't manage what you can't measure.

If you take nothing else from this book, at least get your head around PPC and start generating more leads than you ever thought possible.

Go to Google adwords and take a free tour.

➢ Direct Mail

That's right, snail mail – it's still an effective medium for marketing. At a fraction of the price of employing a salesperson you can put your message in front of hundreds or thousands of prospects on a regular basis.

During a day, your salesperson can only have a face-to-face conversation or telephone conversation with a limited number of potential customers. Using direct mail you can send exactly the right sales message to your target audience – and you can send it to thousands of people at the same time.

As with any piece of direct-response marketing, you must grab the reader's attention with a good headline, create interest and desire through strong benefit statements and then incentivise the reader to take action. Forget all about "brand awareness", with direct mail you're seeking a direct response.

> "What does sexy underwear and a good headline have in common?"

Question: "What does sexy underwear and a good headline have in common?"

Answer: They both grab your attention.

That has always stuck in my mind, and maybe it will with you to. (On the other hand, maybe it just says something about me!)

Try this; the acronym A.I.D.A. is the simplest and most effective copywriting formula I have come across. It stands for **A**ttention, **I**nterest, **D**esire, **A**ction. Use this formula to structure your letters and all other collateral material.

- **Attention** – How will you solve your customers' problems?
- **Interest** – deliver more compelling benefits to back up the headline.
- **Desire** – create a reason that your prospect will want what you have.
- **Action** – Tell them what to do next, how to order, or where to call.

As a business owner, you know more about your product or service than anyone else. Learn to write powerful sales copy that encapsulates all the benefits. All too often I see sales letters which are long, drawn-out, and plain boring. Some letters start with a feeble headline and just go nowhere – that's not sexy underwear! These are letters that are full of information about the company or features of the product without a benefit statement in sight, let alone a call to action.

If we were sitting face-to-face, and you have two minutes to tell me why I should buy your product, I doubt very much that you would give me your company history, so why do people do it in a sales letter? As with e-mail correspondence, I'm a big advocate that sales letters should be professional and conversational, not stuffy or subservient.

Here is a list of power words used by professional copywriters that are proven to get results. See how you can weave them into your sales letters for the greatest effect.

Absolutely, Amazing, Action, Approved, Attractive, Authentic, At Last, Announcing, Advice, Astonishing, Attention
Bargain, Beautiful, Better, Big, Bonus, Break Through
Colourful, Colossal, Complete, Confidential, Controversial, Crammed
Delivered, Direct, Discount, Discover
Easily, Endorsed, Enormous, Essential, Excellent, Exciting, Exclusive, Expert, Extraordinary, Explosive, Extreme
Famous, Fascinating, Fortune, Free, Full, First Time Ever, Fantastic
Genuine, Gift, Gigantic, Greatest, Guaranteed
Helpful, Highest, Huge, Hurry, How to…
Immediately, Immense, Improved, Incredible, Informative, Instant, Instructive, Intense, Interesting, Introducing
Largest, Latest, Lavishly, Lifetime, Liberal, Limited, Love, Lowest, Lucky, Last Chance
Magic, Mammoth, Mega, Miracle

New, Noted, Novel, Now, Never-before
Odd, Outstanding, Opportunity, Offer
Personalized, Popular, Powerful, Practical, Professional, Profitable, Profusely, Proven, Priority, Premium, Phenomenal
Quality, Quickly
Rare, Reduced, Refundable, Remarkable, Reliable, Revealing, Revolutionary, Rush
Secret, Scarce, Secure, Security, Selected, Sense, Sensational, Simplified, Sizeable, Special, Startling, Strange, Strong, Sturdy, Suave, Successful, Superior, Surprising, Save, Send no Money
Terrific, Tested, Tremendous, The Truth About, Today, Time Sensitive
Undeniably, Unconditional, Unique, Unlimited, Unparalleled, Unsurpassed, Unusual, Useful, Urgent
Valuable
Warm, Wealth, Weird, Wonderful, Win, Why, Who Else, Wanted
You, Your, Yes

Once you've written your sales letter, check it against A.I.D.A.

Does it really focus on your customers' needs, wants, and desires? Have you managed to avoid the use of industry jargon or technical details? Are you talking in benefits rather than features? Does it talk to your customer and their needs and not about you or your company?

A well-written sales letter can deliver phenomenal results – direct mail works very effectively.

➤ Business Cards

Everybody I know in business carries a business card. Make sure yours is crisp and clear and easy to read. A simple tip to maximise the effectiveness of a business card is to print both sides. Name and address and contact information on the front and a call to action on the back.

For example, the reverse of my business cards, reads:

> *How do you find more clients, increase sales and improve profits?*
>
> *Download your free report now...*
>
> *10 simple marketing strategies you can implement*
>
> *today to significantly improve your profits!*
>
> *www.eurekasales.co.uk*

Why would you not print on the back of your card?

➢ **Referrals**

I said earlier that if you are relying upon referrals as your single source of lead generation, it was a very high risk, if not a foolish strategy in today's economy – I stand by that.

However, it is an element of your Multi-Faceted Marketing Machine that you should cultivate. The problem is that this kind of word-of-mouth marketing can be slow and unpredictable if left to its own devices. As with every other element of your marketing, you must have a strategy for gaining referrals.

One of the best things about referrals, as you may well know if you've relied on this strategy in the past, is that it's much easier to sell to someone that comes to you via a personal recommendation of one of their friends.

There is one sure-fire way of speeding up the referral process – ask for them!

Now, you may be one of those people that loathe the idea of asking for referrals, but rest assured, this is one of your cheapest and most effective forms of marketing. If done correctly, you can create a stream of regular enquiries at next to no cost.

Before you go asking for referrals, you must make sure that your product or service is regarded in the most positive light by your existing customers. They should be "mad keen fans" rather than merely pleased to have done business with you. Make it your job to find things about your company, service, or products that people want to talk about. Give them an experience (and a good one, not bad) that they simply have to tell their friends about.

The key to getting lots of good referrals is down to the way that you ask for them. If you simply ask, "Do you know anyone that would like to buy my products?" The answer you'll almost certainly get is, "Let me have a think about it and I'll let you know." And the chances that you ever hear back from that person are slim to none.

Providing you have built a good rapport with your customer, and they are extremely satisfied with your product, you can afford to be more direct. You can ask, "Who do you think would benefit from my product?" Ask specifically for their name and contact information. Depending upon the situation, it might even be appropriate for you to ask your customer there and then if they wouldn't mind giving their friend a quick call and introducing you to them.

In addition to asking for referrals, one at a time and face-to-face you might introduce one or all of the following methods:

- **Send a letter** – Write to your existing database explaining that you're looking to find more good quality customers just like them. In the letter, remind them of the benefits of doing business with you and ask for referrals.

- **Provide a guarantee** – By offering a guarantee of satisfaction you're letting your customers know that they're not putting anyone at risk by referring them to you.

- **Reward referrals** – You might want to add a bonus, incentive or discount off their next purchase for anyone providing you with referrals. Don't keep this a secret.

- **Train your staff** – Ensure that all of your team

understand the importance and effectiveness of referrals. You could run your own incentive with your staff to see who can generate the highest level of referrals in a week or a month.

- Above all else, and in keeping with all of your marketing efforts, you must **test and measure** the results of each element of your referral process so that you can continue to improve performance.

➢ Joint Ventures

Another way of increasing referrals and word-of-mouth recommendations is to find various partners with whom you can form a joint venture. You might look for partners with synergistic products. Find a partner who has credibility and a great reputation. That way you can promote their products to your database and vice versa, providing it's relevant and adds value to customers and prospects on your database of course.

➢ Networking

There are numerous networking opportunities available in the business arena. I'm not talking exclusively here about what I call the "Monday moaning meetings". The typical breakfast clubs, where business owners regularly get up at the crack of dawn, only to join downbeat, negative individuals who are full of doom and gloom over a greasy breakfast. I don't wish to tar all breakfast meetings with the same brush. Indeed, I recently attended a breakfast meeting with almost 200 business people. The meeting was lively, fast-paced, and fairly inspirational. Everybody that I spoke to was keen to network for all the right reasons; principally, how can we all generate more business... and the breakfast wasn't bad either!

Think also about networking with groups, clubs or societies that may be in need of your products or services. Offer to attend one of their meetings as a guest speaker. However, try to ensure that your speech is not a blatant sales pitch, but provide them with good valuable information. You will gain their trust as the person to come to when they need your products.

➤ Press and Public Relations

What I mean by press and public relations (PR), is working with the media, including print, radio and TV, to achieve positive coverage on your company that will generate new enquiries and prompt old customers to make contact again.

As with all of your marketing strategies, generating good press and publicity requires a proactive approach. There are essentially two ways of generating good PR; hire a PR agency, or do it yourself.

The essence of most of my strategies is low cost or no cost, and therefore I favour the DIY route. Providing you have GP and TE to infinity there will be no better advocate for your own business than you. Therefore, with no disrespect to PR companies, many of whom are very good, I'd suggest you give this a shot and surprise yourself with the results. You don't need to be an outstanding writer to attract media attention, nor should this be a difficult or expensive task.

I interviewed the editor of a regional newspaper in one of my recent tele-seminars. He outlined for my listeners just how difficult it is to find newsworthy items on a daily and weekly basis and his readiness to receive and print items of local or national interest. I know from the feedback I received that this interview opened many people's eyes to just what can be achieved by working with the local media. If you would like a copy of this interview, and many other interviews from my past tele-seminars, they are available on CD – just drop me an e-mail and request your copy. These normally sell for £19.95+VAT, however, as you have purchased my book and clearly want to make a difference in the marketing efforts of your business:

I will happily send you a copy of the CD for free, while stocks last.

My wife is a personal trainer. She offers personal training in the privacy of her own exclusive gym. One item of equipment within her gym is a new "Power Plate"™. This particular piece of equipment had been justifiably making headlines in national papers a short while ago due to the positive health and fitness benefits it delivers, and its popularity amongst many celebrities.

We rode the back of this awareness and sent a very short press release to our local paper reinforcing the benefits of the product and letting them know that this nationwide phenomenon was available locally. She received a half-page article with colour photographs absolutely free! The result – literally hundreds of enquiries, new clients, and even a waiting list!

What have you got to say that's newsworthy? What is there about your products or services that links to an existing story that's already in the media?

Take a moment now to jot down as many newsworthy stories you can think of that you could create, and even come up with some… sexy underwear headlines too.

My Eureka Moments

How to Thrive Not Just Survive...

➢ Testimonials

Sometimes testimonials will just arrive in the mail or in your inbox, and what a difference it can make to your day. We all want to hear that we do a good job and make people happy. However, as with everything else, obtaining good testimonials that hit all the right points you'd like them to will require some pro-activity on your part.

Write a list of the key elements of your business that you would like testimonials to reinforce. Discuss this with your staff and determine a list of recent customers that you feel have been particularly happy with these various aspects of your services. You can then call these clients as part of your after sales follow-up service and receive their feedback directly.

Whenever one of your customers says something complimentary about your business, be sure to ask them if you can quote them on that. Get their quote written down and use it, along with their name, title, and company – with their permission of course. If possible, obtain a head and shoulders photo of them too. This will add more weight to their comment when it appears on your website.

➢ Listen to Your Customers

At every opportunity, you should be listening to your customers and prospects. Invite feedback, both positive and negative. Bad businesses have a tendency to either ignore the negative or sweep the issues under the carpet. Yet negative feedback from somebody that had a bad experience offers a tremendous opportunity for you to turn that person into one of your biggest fans. And when you turn somebody around from negative to positive, more often than not you don't just solve the problem that one person had, you open up a floodgate of referrals! Ignore the negatives at your peril.

Always ask for feedback, make sure that you actively listen and respond to what you hear.

"Listen to your customers. Listen to all of their comments."

A restaurant near me recently changed hands and spent a fortune on refurbishment. My wife and I went along for a meal in their opening week. They were busy, which for their sake I was pleased to see. Unfortunately, things didn't go too smoothly. The wrong starters were delivered to the table. The main course took so long to arrive that we had finished a bottle of wine by the time it finally came, and it too was the wrong order. No problem, opening week, we decided to give them another try.

A few weeks later I called to make another booking. I asked for a table at 8.30 p.m. The person on the other end of the phone asked if I could make it 7.45 p.m. instead, as they had a large group arriving at 8.30 p.m. They went on to explain that if I made it 7.45 p.m., we would get quicker service, and so I agreed.

We arrived at 7.45 and had ordered our meals before eight. By 8.45, We had still not received our starters. When they eventually arrived, our hot starters were only just lukewarm. Our main courses took another three quarters of an hour. One order was incorrect, and the other was almost cold. Not a great evening.

As our plates were being cleared by a less-than-enthusiastic waiter, the owner of the restaurant walked towards our table, and without breaking stride looked towards us and asked, "Was everything OK?" she smiled a fake smile and walked on without waiting for a response. The bill arrived without a comment card to obtain our feedback, let alone build their database.

I was prepared to give them just one more shot, but unfortunately, it was three strikes and you're out. Our third and last visit showed absolutely no improvement, but more importantly to me it demonstrated the complacency of a badly run business. We won't return. If you and I do get to meet face-to-face in the future, I will happily make a recommendation – one restaurant not to visit in my area.

Listen to your customers. Listen to all of their comments, good and bad, and then take appropriate action. These comments will help you grow your business.

So **MFMM** stands for a **Multi-Faceted Marketing Machine**. I hope that you will understand the importance to your businesses success of moving from the over-reliance on a single marketing strategy to becoming a successful **Multi-Faceted Marketing Machine**.

None of these strategies of one-off events. For your continued success they require **Regular Repeat A**ction, which you **T**est and **M**easure. By doing this, you will create a strong healthy **P**ipeline of **S**ales **L**eads.

Summary

MFMM + RRA (TM!) = PSL

Multi-Faceted Marketing Machine + Regular Repeat Action (Test and Measure!) = Pipeline of Sales Leads

- Develop an arsenal of simple marketing methodologies.
- Don't expect an avalanche of sales leads from one single source, or one single occasion. You need regular repeat action in order to succeed.
- Stop wasting your money on advertising that doesn't work. Remember, you can't manage what you can't measure.
- Forget "brand awareness", go for direct response marketing.
- What does sexy underwear and a good headline have in common?
- A.I.D.A. – be bold, don't be boring.
- Learn to write powerful sales copy and strong headlines.
- The golden rule – test and measure

QL x CR = STC + MFMM = STHC ≥1

Qualified Lead x Conversion Ratio = Sale To Customer + Multi-Faceted Marketing Machine = Sale To Happy Customer greater than or equal to one.

Whilst the definition of a qualified lead changes from company to company (and rightly so), let me give you my definition of a generally "qualified" lead. By this I mean a potential customer who has expressed an interest in your product or service. I don't simply mean everybody on your database or the database of one of your joint-venture partners.

These prospects may have been in contact you directly by phone or in person. They may have responded to an advertisement or a piece of editorial in a newspaper, or indeed any one of your Multi-Faceted Marketing Machine strategies.

It's important to establish whether your prospect has the appropriate budget or means of financing available to make the required purchase. Does the person you're talking to actually have the authority to authorise the purchase? Do they really want or maybe even really need what you have on offer, and that they want it within an acceptable timeframe? If you can answer yes to these questions, then in my book you have a quality lead and a prospect rather than just a suspect, a maybe some day, maybe not kind of a lead.

Now you need to establish what your conversion ratio is. How many of your **Q**uality **L**eads do you successfully convert into a sale? Is it 1 in 5, 1 in 10, 1 in 100?

This is a really important part of your strategic planning. Hopefully, you are working towards your written, daily, weekly, monthly, quarterly and annual sales targets. Understanding the importance of this key metric will help you plan all of your sales and marketing efforts effectively allowing you to achieve your goals. For example:

- How much do you want to earn from your business in the next 12 months?
- On average, how much profit do you make per sale?
- So how many sales do you need at that profit level to achieve your goal?
- What's your conversion rate of qualified leads to a sale?
- At that rate of conversion, how many leads do you need?
- How many qualified leads are you currently generating?

One very powerful question you should be asking yourself is what can you do to improve your conversion ratio?

Almost immediately, people want to answer that question by suggesting they hone their sales skills, or those of their sales force. Naturally, this can only improve things. However, I want to offer you the following piece of advice: <u>the number one way to dramatically improve your conversion ratio is to do just one thing</u>...**FOLLOW UP!**

It's that simple. If you want to see a massive uplift in your conversion ratio, simply follow up your leads

It's that simple, and yet 49% of businesses <u>never</u> follow-up. Why? I have heard all sorts of excuses:

- We don't want to appear like pushy salespeople
- We don't want to bother our clients
- We simply don't have the hours of the day

The list goes on...

A further 25% of businesses only ever make a second call. You can then refer to the list above. Again, we don't want to appear like pushy salespeople, blah blah blah – all feeble excuses for not running an effective sales process.

> **"Hopefully, you are working towards your written, daily, weekly, monthly, quarterly and annual sales targets."**

If you are a member of the 49% club, those that never follow up, here's a number that could and should make you think again.

Only 2% of sales are made on first contact. Now my maths isn't great, but if only 2% of sales are being made on first contact, and you're one of those people that do not follow up, that means that 98% of the available business is being left on the table.

You've done the hard work, you've generated the enquiry, and you've produced a qualified lead. If you don't have the manpower and you don't have the hours in the day, fine – automate your systems; this is a perfect application for an auto responder. Create a follow-up system to feed useful and valuable information to your prospects that will help them come to their decision in your favour.

I don't mean a follow-up system adopted by weak or inexperienced salespeople. The sort of follow-up system that consists of nothing more than annoying phone calls to ask "have you made your mind up yet, have you made your mind up yet, have you made your mind up yet." You get the picture, pretty annoying, and this is never going get the result you want.

> **"The number one way to dramatically improve your conversion ratio is to do just one thing… FOLLOW UP!"**

How many times do you follow up? Here are some more statistics that I hope will open your eyes and your minds:

- 49% of businesses never follow up
- 25% only ever make a second contact
- 2% of sales are made on first contact
- 3% are made on second contact
- 5% on third contact
- 10% on fourth
- 80% take between 5 and 12 contacts!

To dramatically improve your conversion rates, you must build an effective follow-up system. I know for a fact that less people would moan about how bad business is or how badly they're affected by recession if they only had an effective 10 to 25-step follow-up process in place. If business doesn't dramatically pick up after taking these steps, I would question whether you ever had a viable business to start with.

So a **Q**ualified **L**ead x **C**onversion **R**atio = **S**ale **T**o **C**ustomer. When you add to this the various elements of your **M**ulti-**F**aceted **M**arketing **M**achine, you can achieve a **S**ale **T**o **H**appy **C**ustomer greater than or equal to one.

Too many business owners still simply focus on making a sale. Smart, and very often wealthy, entrepreneurs make a sale to get a customer. These smart entrepreneurs have moved their business away from a one-off transactional sale to nurturing and building long-lasting relationships.

Selling to an existing happy customer is far less expensive and an awful lot easier than selling to new customers every single time. But you absolutely must ensure your existing customer base knows the extent and breadth of your product range and not leave it to chance for them to find that you could have supplied the product that they just bought elsewhere.

> *"I was at your seminar at Essex University two weeks ago – you inspired me. You really spoke to me when you said how we needed to keep in mind what we can offer existing customers as well as reaching out to new ones. Within 10 minutes of sending my newsletter (through Constant Contact), I had an e-mail from an ex-client I haven't seen for over a year. I am confident she will return as a client, and she is likely*

to spend around £1000 with me over the next 3 months – nice! So, thanks, Steve."

– Judy Hoskins

Lighter Life Counsellor, Leigh on Sea

Assuming you have 10 products available in your portfolio, how many of your products could each customer benefit from. Your database should be capable of recording how many of your products you have sold to your customers and how many times you have told them about the benefits of those products. You should be recording and measuring your rate of "Told to Sold".

If you don't have a sophisticated CRM database, don't worry. Start a simple spreadsheet that lists your clients and prospects down one column. Along the top of the spreadsheet list all of the products you have available for sale. Along the line of each client enter "told" or "sold" by each product and you will soon see a picture emerging of where you need to spend some marketing activity that will produce results for you.

Company	Product 1	Product 2	Product 3	Product 4
BCD & Co	Sold	Told x 1		Sold
EFG & Co.	Sold		Told x 1	Told x 3
HIJ & Co.	Sold	Sold		Sold
LMN & Co	Told x 1			Sold

Assuming the products above are of similar value, where would you spend your marketing efforts next?

We have very light-coloured carpets in our house which require regular professional cleaning. Thankfully, we have found ourselves an excellent local cleaning guy. He's not cheap, but he is very good.

At one of his last visits I asked whether he cleaned curtains too. Unfortunately he didn't, but had he thought to establish a joint venture with a curtain-cleaning business, he could have taken an order that day – that's how much we trust and respect him.

It was purely by chance that I discovered another cleaning service he had available besides carpets (but he hadn't informed me of). We were standing in my kitchen as I cut him a cheque for the carpet cleaning, and he mentioned how much he liked our new orangery, which was a new extension to the kitchen. I explained to him that the only regret I had was that the limestone floor that runs from the kitchen and had been extended into the orangery showed distinct differences in their age having been bought and laid several years apart.

Only then did he mention that he could clean limestone floors too! And what a job he did! You would never guess the floor had been laid at different times – it all looked like new when he'd finished. My hope is that I can repay him now by teaching him how to work on his business and not just in it. The repayment will be 100 times more than he will bank from cleaning my carpets and floors!

Don't keep your products or services a secret from existing clients or new prospects!

Summary

$$QL \times CR = STC + MFMM = STHC \geq 1$$

Qualified Lead x Conversion Ratio = Sale To Customer + Multi-Faceted Marketing Machine = Sale To Happy Customer greater than or equal to one.

- What is your conversion ratio?
- How can you improve the ratio?
- Follow up!
- 49% of businesses never follow up
- 25% only ever make a second contact
- 80% take between 5 and 12 contacts!
- How many of your different products or services could each customer benefit from?
- It is far easier to sell to an existing happy customer – and less expensive – but what are you doing about it?
- Develop a 10 to 25-step follow-up process.

Unless you have developed a 10 to 25-stage follow-up process, and you're still not getting results, don't tell me your businesses is suffering because of the recession!

(TM + TM = BR) BR = MP + MLBW ∞)

Test and Measure + Test and Measure = Better Results

Better Results = More Profit + More of the Life and Business you Want to Infinity

➤ Testing and Measuring

This is essential for any business. If you're not testing and measuring everything you do, how do you know what's working and what's not?

A client of mine historically had taken advertising space in the yellow pages at a cost of £1800 pa because... well... it was worth a go in their minds. Did they get any business from it? They didn't know. They had no system in place to test and measure, they just assumed it was worthwhile.

To my horror, during one of our coaching sessions I discovered they had decided to renew their add campaign with yellow pages again, but this time at a reduced rate of £995 as they were a repeat customer! Repeat offender more like! I now try to make it very clear to anyone in business: if you can't test and measure the results of marketing efforts, don't waste your money on it.

This was a small family-run business. The owners had not had the time or money available for a proper family holiday for years. No testing and no measuring, it was quite mad. I imagine they could have had a lovely holiday with all the money they wasted on advertising in this way.

The Japanese, masters of testing, have a great word for this – Kaizen, which translated means "constant and never-ending improvement". In plain English I like to think of this as – Plan – do – check – review. Whichever version you can relate to, remember it and practice it.

"In order to get there, you need to test everything. It will be worth it."

Through testing and measuring, you know which adds to run and which ones to drop, which marketing strategies to stick with, which need changing and fine-tuning, or which ones to drop. There is no point at all continuing to do the same thing and just hoping for a better result.

You need to know where you stand before you start and have the ability to measure results along the way. Plan – do – check – review. Are you getting the desired effect and results from your marketing efforts? Fine-tune, redirect or dump them before they cost you too much time and money and have the exact opposite effect from what you wanted in the first place.

How would the client I mentioned above know where their leads come from? They didn't have time to conduct the analysis; they were busy with… "stuff". Learn to "block out" time to work on things that are important to your business. Block out time as the business owner to allow you to test and measure – is it important? No, it's imperative!

The true secret to generating profits (and not just sales) is delivering the **right** product to the **right** customer with the **right** ad using the **right** medium at the **right** time – but, I hear you say, all of that can take time, effort and, of course, money. In order to get there, you need to test everything. It will be worth it.

You need to test new product ideas, try new media both online and offline to target your key message, and test out new strategies. You can even try different headlines, subject lines, copy lengths, target markets, offers, prices, etc, etc.

But without properly and quantifiably **tracking, measuring and analysing** your test results, you could simply be losing money, visitors, customers and so much more – from right under your nose!

What do you do? You can use ad-tracking software such as www.hypertracker.com, which in essence will keep track of the results of all manner of ads and campaigns for you – visit their site and take a tour.

A really simple method of measuring the effectiveness of individual adverts or promotions is to register a new domain name for use with that advert alone. Domain name registration is very inexpensive using services like www.123-reg.co.uk or www.ukreg.com. If your main website for example is www.fish-ponds-north-london.co.uk, then just use your company initials and set up a domain name of www.fpnl.co.uk.

You then have your techie or Webmaster set up a "redirect" –

meaning anyone who visits the new domain will automatically be sent to your normal site, but critically, you will be able to keep the exact count of the redirects, and therefore, who came from the advert using your new domain name. You will know exactly how much traffic that advert produced.

In its simplest form, ask every person that contacts you where they heard about you and why they contacted you and – note it down. This truly is not rocket science, is it? Later you can look into other methods of automating this kind of data collection, but for now, just ask the question and ask it every single time.

Plan – do – check – review. Be honest with yourself, work your marketing plan and measure the results. If it's working, fantastic, turn up the heat and measure again. If it's having an adverse effect, dump it. Don't stick with something because you thought it was a good idea; if it doesn't work, jettison it and start over again.

Here are some more key points to test and measure:

- How many new customers do you deal with versus repeat customers?
- How many leads or prospects convert to sales?
- Once a sale is made, how many become repeat clients and for how many more times?
- What else could you sell to your existing customers? This is known as "up-selling" or "add-on selling", and it's a very effective method of increasing profits. You buy a burger at any fast-food place and the kid behind the

counter will ask, "Do you want fries or a drink with that?" Initially you only wanted a burger, but have you any idea how many people will add to their order when asked? Do you think McDonald's and Burger King would keep doing it if they didn't KNOW the results it produces?

To keep doing the same thing and just hoping for different results is the definition of insanity. To obtain different results, you need to make changes.

If you keep doing what you've always done, you're going to get what you've always got. At least that used to be the chant. Forget it. If you keep doing what you've always done, you're going to very likely go out of business. You need to make changes and fast.

Small changes can produce huge results. Look to each change you make as part of your ongoing Profit Improvement Programme. I've come to know and love these changes as **PIP's,** you will too. **PIP**'s – not rocket science, that's what you want – more **PIP**'s. Business just has to be simple, deliverable, and systematic to be most effective and profitable.

The more you Test and Measure, the Better the Results you get. Better the Results = More Profit, and the more profit you make, the More of the Life and Business you Want is yours to infinity.

SUMMARY

(TM + TM = BR) BR = MP + MLBW ∞)

Test and **M**easure + **T**est and **M**easure = **B**etter **R**esults

Better **R**esults = **M**ore **P**rofit + **M**ore of the **L**ife and **B**usiness you **W**ant to Infinity

- What's the golden rule of marketing?
- TEST & MEASURE
- Learn to work **on** your business – not just **in** it
- Set goals
- Plan your work and work your plan
- To keep doing the same things and just hoping for a different result is the definition of insanity
- If you keep doing what you've always done…

This is Your Proven Formula for Business Success

THE BUSINESS SUCCESS FORMULA

$$((GP + TE\,\infty)\,NM + (PPW + MRN) + QP = PO$$
$$AS + LNP = LO + MP = GBM$$
$$MFMM + RRA\,(TM!) = PSL$$
$$QL \times CR = STC + MFMM = STHC \geq 1$$
$$(TM + TM = BR)\,BR = MP + MLBW\,\infty)$$

©Eureka Sales Solutions Ltd 2009

It's OK… it's not rocket science,

But it is your proven formula for business success

SIMPLE!

Your Extra Special Reader's Bonus

There's only one thing that is constant in our world – that's change.

The pace of change in today's climate is faster then ever, so our ability to anticipate and manage change is constantly being tested. Everyone needs to develop a sense of urgency (not panic), which challenges complacency within organisations at every level. **Adapt and change in a timely fashion, and you will win** – fail to make changes and you will very likely sink.

There are three ways to make changes in your sales strategy that will make the bad times for others completely irrelevant to you and your business as you continue to thrive, and not just survive in any economy.

I am willing to share these three secrets and much more with you. I am running a series of special one-day sales and marketing master classes to explain all, and you are invited.

In fact, as you have already purchased and read this book, **you are pre-qualified for a place** at an exceptionally special price.

In just one day you will learn:

- The right questions to ask in order to succeed in business
- How to make lots of money – fast (not a get-rich-quick hoax or scam – this is for real)
- The 10 essential secrets to entrepreneurial success

- Exactly what to offer the top 20% of your customers to explode your sales
- 12 champagne marketing strategies for a beer budget
- The three killer changes to your sales strategy that will create exponential growth in your business.
- Plus much, much more.

You will leave the day with a simple, solid, written action plan for a bright and profitable future – guaranteed.

As someone that's shown they want to make changes and see improvements by purchasing this book, I now want to repay you many times over.

SAVE £100.00 plus VAT! People have paid £249 plus VAT for previous courses. Book your place today and you can attend this amazing daylong master class that will transform your business for just £149.00 plus VAT.

I guarantee you will walk away with the tools to generate at least 10 times the cost of your course or you pay nothing – absolutely nothing. If you don't believe you have received valuable information which will deliver on this promise, then I will refund your money in full, no quibble, no questions.

All you have to do is e-mail my office now with the following... **Password BSF109** – we will then let you know the dates and venues for upcoming events. info@eurekasales.co.uk Don't forget to quote the **Password BSF109** and provide us with your correct contact information so we can make a booking for you ASAP.

NEW!

Why don't you join one of my **marketing mentor mastermind groups**, where you will learn new techniques guaranteed to boost your sales and at the same time network with other positive, like-minded entrepreneurs sharing more ideas and concepts that you can benefit from too? Enquire about the nearest group to you right now:

www.yoursalesdirector.co.uk/events.

If you want more information, just call my office on

0845 053 4937 today.

All the best,

Steve Clarke – Your "Virtual" Sales Director

P.S. Massive savings available for Federation of Small Businesses (FSB) Members and attendees of my past "Beat the Recession – Boost Your Sales" Seminars'. Check rates and availability at www.yoursalesdirector.co.uk/events now!

Federation of Small Businesses
The UK's Leading Business Organisation